My First Animal Library

Caribou

by Cari Meister

Bullfrog Books

Ideas for Parents and Teachers

Bullfrog Books let children practice reading informational text at the earliest reading levels. Repetition, familiar words, and photo labels support early readers.

Before Reading

- Discuss the cover photo. What does it tell them?

- Look at the picture glossary together. Read and discuss the words.

Read the Book

- "Walk" through the book and look at the photos. Let the child ask questions. Point out the photo labels.

- Read the book to the child, or have him or her read independently.

After Reading

- Prompt the child to think more. Ask: Have you ever seen a caribou?

Bullfrog Books are published by Jump!
5357 Penn Avenue South
Minneapolis, MN 55419
www.jumplibrary.com

Copyright © 2019 Jump! International copyright reserved in all countries. No part of this book may be reproduced in any form without written permission from the publisher.

Library of Congress Cataloging-in-Publication Data

Names: Meister, Cari, author.
Title: Caribou / by Cari Meister.
Description: Minneapolis, MN : Jump!, 2018.
Series: My first animal library | Series: Bullfrog books | Includes index. | Audience: Ages 5 to 8.
Audience: Grades K to 3.
Identifiers: LCCN 2017040243 (print) | LCCN 2017043177 (ebook) | ISBN 9781624967535 (ebook)
ISBN 9781624967528 (hardcover : alk. paper)
Subjects: LCSH: Caribou—Juvenile literature.
Classification: LCC QL737.U55 (ebook)
LCC QL737.U55 M369 2018 (print) | DDC 599.65/8—dc23
LC record available at https://lccn.loc.gov/20170402438

Editor: Jenna Trnka
Book Designer: Leah Sanders

Photo Credits: Iakov Filimonov/Shutterstock, cover, 22, 24; Sylvie Bouchard/Shutterstock, 1; Gagat55/Shutterstock, 3; Minden Pictures/SuperStock, 4; lightpix/iStock, 5; Rumo/Adobe Stock, 6–7; YinYang/iStock, 7; Eric Isselee/Shutterstock, 8; Shin Yoshino/Minden Pictures/SuperStock, 8–9, 23bl; Michio Hoshino/Minden Pictures/SuperStock, 10–11, 23tr; longtaildog/Shutterstock, 12; Carlos Charlez/Shutterstock, 13; Donald M. Jones/Minden Pictures/SuperStock, 14–15; Chris Hill/Adobe Stock, 16–17; Manuel Lacoste/Shutterstock, 18; Jeff McGraw/Shutterstock, 19; Mark Raycroft/Minden Pictures/SuperStock, 20–21; Kris Grabiec/Shutterstock, 23tl; Evgeniia Ozerkina/Shutterstock, 23br.

Printed in the United States of America at Corporate Graphics in North Mankato, Minnesota.

Table of Contents

On the Move

A caribou digs in the snow.

What is it looking for?
Food.

hoof

Each hoof is big.

It is like a shovel.

A caribou is a kind of deer.

It is a herbivore.

It eats plants.

deer

Caribou live
in big herds.

Some are bigger
than 500,000!

They travel far
each year.

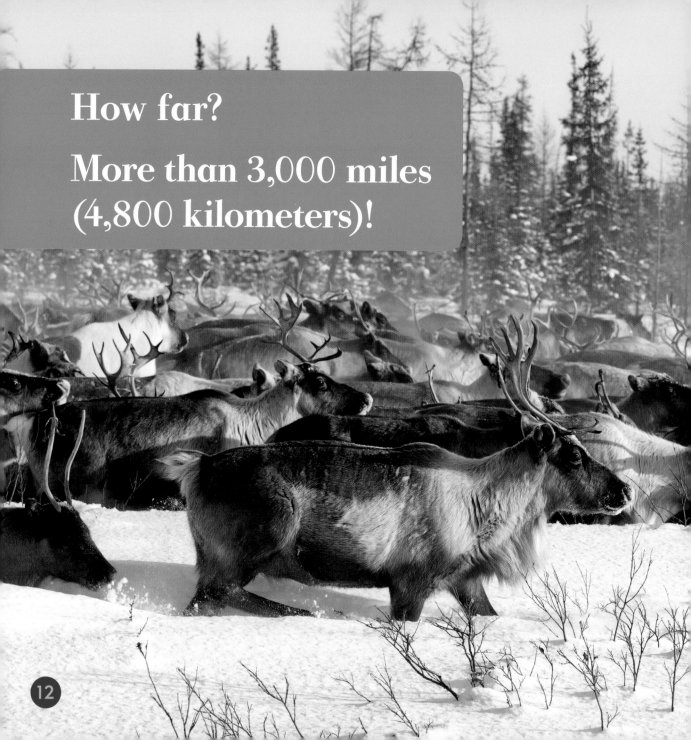

How far?

More than 3,000 miles
(4,800 kilometers)!

Why?
To find food.

food

They live in
the Arctic.

It is very cold.

Not much grows.

They have a special bone.

It is in their nose.

It warms the air.

fur

These deer have thick fur.

antlers

They have
big antlers.

Males use them
to fight.

Wow!

They will shed
them in winter.

Parts of a Caribou

antlers
Both male and female caribou use their antlers for digging. Males use them to fight for females.

fur
Thick fur keeps caribou warm in cold temperatures.

muzzle
A special bone in the muzzle warms the cold air caribou breathe in.

hooves
Large, hollow hooves help caribou paddle through water, dig snow, and walk on ice.

Picture Glossary

Arctic
The area around the North Pole.

herds
Large groups of animals that live and travel together.

herbivore
An animal that only eats plants.

shed
To lose or get rid of.

Index

To Learn More

Learning more is as easy as 1, 2, 3.

1) Go to www.factsurfer.com

2) Enter "caribou" into the search box.

3) Click the "Surf" button to see a list of websites.

With factsurfer.com, finding more information is just a click away.